The Countries

Norway

Tamara L. Britton
ABDO Publishing Company

visit us at
www.abdopub.com

Published by ABDO Publishing Company, 4940 Viking Drive, Edina, Minnesota 55435.
Copyright © 2003 by Abdo Consulting Group, Inc. International copyrights reserved in
all countries. No part of this book may be reproduced in any form without written
permission from the publisher.

Printed in the United States.

Photo Credits: Corbis
Contributing Editors: Kristin Van Cleaf, Stephanie Hedlund
Art Direction & Maps: Neil Klinepier

Library of Congress Cataloging-in-Publication Data

Britton, Tamara L., 1963-
    Norway / Tamara L. Britton.
        p. cm. -- (The countries)
    Includes index.
    ISBN 1-57765-839-6
    1. Norway--Juvenile literature. 2. Norway. I. Title. II. Series.

DL409 .B75 2002
948.1--dc21
                                                    2002020752

Contents

God Dag!

Hello from Norway! Norway is Europe's fifth-largest country. It lies on the Scandinavian **Peninsula**, near the Arctic Circle. Part of Norway is so far north, the sun does not set for weeks at a time!

Most of Norway's people speak Norwegian and practice the Lutheran religion. Almost all Norwegians can read and write. Norway has a strong **economy** and its people are well educated. These factors mean most Norwegians enjoy a high standard of living.

A king or queen and a **parliament** make up Norway's government. The Norwegian government provides extensive social service programs. These programs provide health care, housing assistance, social security, and family assistance. All of these things make Norway a great home for its people.

God dag *from Norway!*

Fast Facts

OFFICIAL NAME: Kingdom of Norway
  (Kongeriket Norge)
CAPITAL: Oslo

LAND
- Area: 125,181 square miles (324,220 sq km)
- Mountain Range: Long Mountains
- Highest Point: Galdhø Peak 8,100 feet (2,469 m)
- Lowest Point: Norwegian Sea (sea level)
- Major River: Glåma River
- Major Lake: Lake Mjøsa

PEOPLE
- Population: 4,503,440 (July 2001 est.)
- Major Cities: Oslo, Bergen
- Languages: Norwegian, Sami
- Religions: Protestantism, Catholicism

GOVERNMENT
- Form: Constitutional monarchy
- Head of State: King or queen
- Head of Government: Prime minister
- Legislature: Parliament
- Flag: Blue cross outlined in white on a red field. The
  vertical part of the cross is along the mast side.
- National Anthem: "Ja, vi elsker dette landet"
  ("Norway, thine is our devotion")
- Nationhood: Independence from Sweden 1905

ECONOMY
- Agricultural Products: Barley, potatoes; cattle, pigs, fish
- Mining Products: Petroleum, natural gas
- Manufactured Products: Aluminum, paper, furniture,
  electronic products
- Money: Krone (1 krone = 100 øre)

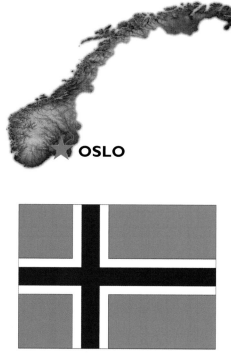

OSLO

Norway's flag

Norwegian kroner

Timeline

3000 B.C.	Migrants settle in Norway
A.D. 800s	Vikings raid and conquer neighboring lands; Harald I becomes Norway's first king
1349	Black Death kills two-thirds of Norway's population
1387-1388	Margaret I becomes queen of Norway, Denmark, and Sweden; adopts Erik of Pomerania as her heir
1397	Erik of Pomerania crowned king of all three countries, creating the Union of Kalmar
1523	Union of Kalmar ends
1536	Denmark declares Norway a Danish province
1814	Denmark gives Norway to Sweden in Treaty of Kiel; Norwegians write their own constitution
1905	Norway becomes independent; Haakon VII is king
1939-1945	World War II; German troops invade and occupy Norway
1972	Norwegians reject joining the European Union
1977	Gro Harlem Brundtland is elected Norway's first female prime minister
1991	Harald V becomes Norway's third king since independence
1994	Norwegians reject membership in European Union for second time

History

People have lived in Norway for nearly 10,000 years. About 3000 B.C., migrant peoples settled in Norway. They grew barley and raised cows and sheep.

Around A.D. 800, Scandinavian Vikings set out to raid and conquer neighboring settlements. On one of these missions, Erik the Red brought the first settlers to Greenland. Some historians believe his son, Leif Eriksson (LAAV ER-ihk-suhn), made the first European voyage to North America.

Harald I took control of Norway's western coast in the late ninth century. He became Norway's first king. In 1015, Olaf II Haraldsson became king of all of Norway. He established Christianity as Norway's religion.

Vikings land near neighboring settlements

The Viking period ended in the late 1000s. The Viking retreat caused political and social confusion. Regional leaders struggled to claim the throne.

The people fought many civil wars until 1217. That year, Haakon (HAW-kuhn) IV became king and restored peace. In 1349, the **Black Death** struck Norway. It killed nearly two-thirds of the population.

In 1355, Haakon VI became Norway's king. His wife, Margaret, was the daughter of King Valdemar IV of Denmark. When Valdemar died, Margaret's young son Olaf became king of Denmark. Margaret ruled as **regent**.

Queen Margaret I

When Haakon VI died in 1380, Olaf became king of Norway, too. Margaret was also Norway's **regent**. Olaf died in 1387, and Margaret became queen. That same year, she adopted her nephew, Erik of Pomerania. In 1388, Swedish noblemen elected Margaret to rule Sweden, too.

In 1389, Erik was named Margaret's heir (AIR) in Norway. In 1397, he became king of Sweden, Norway, and Denmark. This created the Union of Kalmar.

The union lasted until 1523. In 1536, Denmark declared Norway a Danish **province**. Norway's government lost much of its power. But Norwegians continued to think about independence.

In 1807, many European countries fought in the Napoleonic Wars. Denmark and France fought against Great Britain and Sweden. During the fighting, Norway was isolated by a British blockade. The blockade meant Norwegians could begin managing their own affairs. But in 1813, Sweden defeated Denmark.

In 1814, Denmark gave Norway to Sweden in the Treaty of Kiel. But Norwegians did not accept the treaty. They wrote their own **constitution**. So Sweden attacked Norway. After 14 days of fighting, Norway was forced to accept Swedish rule. But Norwegians were able to keep their constitution.

In 1905, Norwegians voted for independence. Sweden's King Oscar II agreed to give up control of Norway. Then Norwegians voted Denmark's Prince Charles to rule Norway as King Haakon VII.

King Haakon VII

Gro Harlem Brundtland

When **World War II** began in 1939, Norway's government declared itself **neutral**. But in 1940, German troops invaded Norway. They occupied the country throughout the war.

After the war ended in 1945, Norway became a member of the United Nations. In 1949, Norway's government also joined the North Atlantic Treaty Organization.

In 1972, Norwegians rejected a treaty to join the European Union. They were worried their government might lose power in another union. The people rejected joining again in 1994.

Norwegian voters elected Gro Harlem Brundtland (BROONT-lahn) as Norway's first female **prime minister** in 1977. In 1990, the government amended the **constitution** to allow women to be the monarch in Norway. Harald V became king in 1991. He is Norway's third king since the country's independence.

Today, Norway has a strong **economy** supported by **petroleum** exports. Its liberal social services create a genuine system of **social democracy**. Norway's beautiful land, successful economy, and progressive social services system offer much for its people.

King Harald V and his wife, Queen Sonja

Norway's Land

Norway is on the western side of the Scandinavian **Peninsula**. It shares this rocky land with Sweden. Norway is bordered on the north by the Barents Sea, and on the west by the Norwegian and North Seas. The Skager Strait forms Norway's southern border. Sweden, Finland, and Russia join Norway on the east.

Norway has around 1,700 glaciers. Jostedals (YO-steh-dahls) Glacier is the largest ice field in Europe outside of Iceland. Norway's land holds about 160,000 lakes. Much of its western shore is cut by steep and narrow **fjords** (fee-AWRDZ).

Norway has a temperate climate. The coast and southern part of the country have cool summers and mild winters. Inland, summers are warmer and winters are colder. Norway also experiences frequent gales and weather changes.

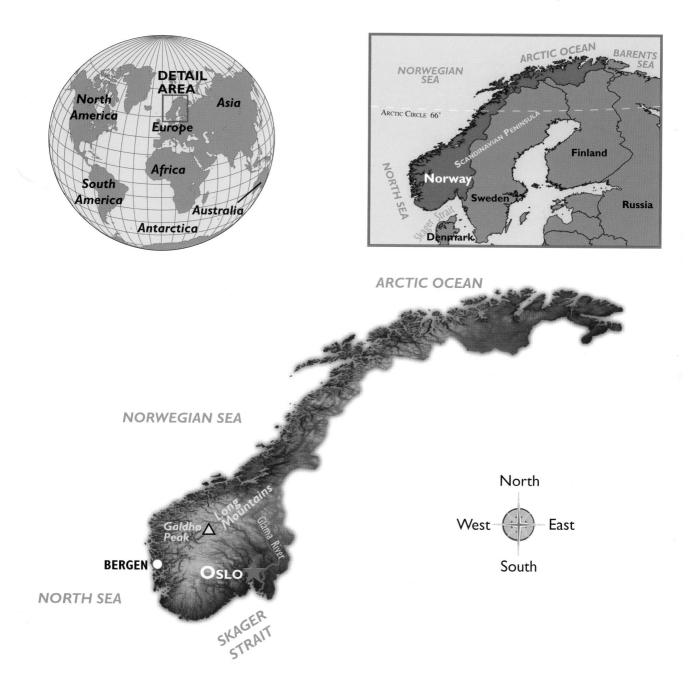

DETAIL AREA

North America

Asia

Europe

Africa

South America

Australia

Antarctica

NORWEGIAN SEA

ARCTIC OCEAN

BARENTS SEA

ARCTIC CIRCLE 66°

SCANDINAVIAN PENINSULA

Finland

NORTH SEA

Norway

Sweden

Russia

Skager Strait

Denmark

ARCTIC OCEAN

NORWEGIAN SEA

North

West — East

South

Long Mountains

Galdhø Peak

Glama River

BERGEN

OSLO

NORTH SEA

SKAGER STRAIT

Northern Norway is called the Land of the Midnight Sun. From mid-May to the end of July, the sun does not set. But in the winter, the sun does not rise from the end of November to the end of January.

The Geiranerfjord was formed when glaciers scraped the bottom of the sea, carving a deep trench. The glaciers then melted, creating the fjord.

Rain

Summer

Winter

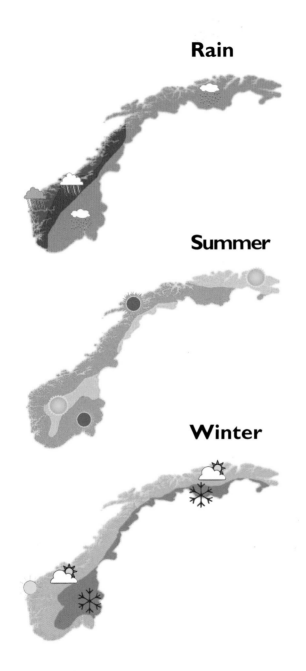

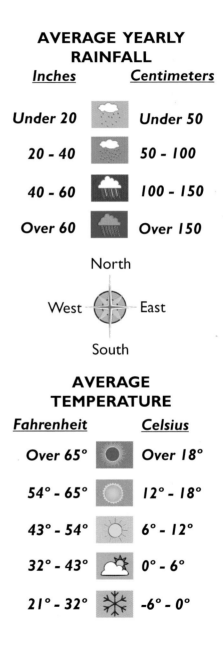

AVERAGE YEARLY RAINFALL

Inches		*Centimeters*
Under 20		*Under 50*
20 - 40		*50 - 100*
40 - 60		*100 - 150*
Over 60		*Over 150*

North

West — East

South

AVERAGE TEMPERATURE

Fahrenheit		*Celsius*
Over 65°		*Over 18°*
54° - 65°		*12° - 18°*
43° - 54°		*6° - 12°*
32° - 43°		*0° - 6°*
21° - 32°		*-6° - 0°*

Plants & Animals

Thick, **coniferous** forests of spruce and pine trees grow in Norway's mountains. **Deciduous** (dih-SIH-juh-wuhs) forests of oak, ash, elm, and maple trees grow in the lower elevations. Dwarf birch and willow trees grow above 28,000 feet (8,534 m).

Wild berries are abundant throughout Norway. Blueberries, cranberries, and cloudberries are most common. Cloudberry plants have yellow berries. They are often found in Scandinavia and Great Britain.

Elk, wolverine, lemming, and reindeer (RAYN-dihr) live in Norway. Lemming are small, mouse-like animals that live in northern areas. In Norway, they will sometimes swarm. Lemming groups will cover large areas of land while searching for food.

Reindeer are also called caribou. Both males and females have antlers. They stand about 4 feet (1 m) tall and weigh about 660 pounds (299 kg). Their coats can be black or white, but most reindeer are gray or brown.

Reindeer have big hooves so they can walk on snow. In the winter, they eat lichen. In summer, they eat grass and small trees.

Some Norwegians raise reindeer for their meat, milk, and hides.

The Norwegians

The majority of people in Norway are Norwegian. They speak Norwegian, Norway's official language. Almost all Norwegians practice the Lutheran religion.

The native Sami (SAY-me), or Lapp people, is Norway's largest minority group. Its people often speak one of three Sami languages. Most speak Norwegian, too. Many Sami are Lutherans, though some still practice their traditional religions.

Most Norwegians live in or near urban areas. They usually live in modern apartment buildings. About one-fourth of Norwegians live in rural areas. Wealthy Norwegians have single-family homes. Many are made of wood.

A Norwegian woman in traditional clothing

A table set for a traditional Norwegian lunch

Norway has many traditional foods. For breakfast Norwegians often eat *geitost* (GEIT-oost), a brown cheese made from goat's milk. They also eat pickled herring and a bread called *flatbrød* (FLAT-broe). Norway's location between many seas makes seafood popular. Salmon, cod, and shrimp are among many Norwegians' favorite foods.

Almost every Norwegian can read and write. Norwegian law requires children between 7 and 16 to attend school. Elementary school is followed by secondary school. Then students may attend a technical school or a university preparatory school. For students who decide to go to university, Norway has them in Oslo, Bergen, Trondheim, and Tromsø.

Norway's 30,000 Sami are **seminomads**. They are native to northern Norway, Sweden, Finland, and parts of Russia. Traditionally, they herd reindeer. But today, many Sami people also farm or fish. They live along the seas, rivers, or in mountainous regions.

A Sami man packs hay in his boots. The hay will keep his feet warm during the cold Norwegian winter.

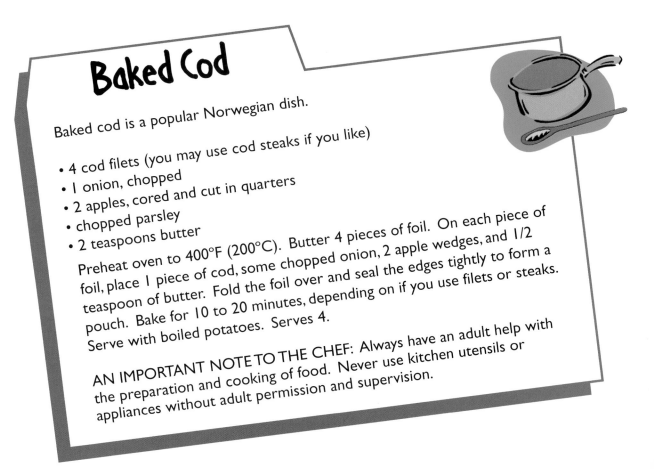

Baked Cod

Baked cod is a popular Norwegian dish.

- 4 cod filets (you may use cod steaks if you like)
- 1 onion, chopped
- 2 apples, cored and cut in quarters
- chopped parsley
- 2 teaspoons butter

Preheat oven to 400°F (200°C). Butter 4 pieces of foil. On each piece of foil, place 1 piece of cod, some chopped onion, 2 apple wedges, and 1/2 teaspoon of butter. Fold the foil over and seal the edges tightly to form a pouch. Bake for 10 to 20 minutes, depending on if you use filets or steaks. Serve with boiled potatoes. Serves 4.

AN IMPORTANT NOTE TO THE CHEF: Always have an adult help with the preparation and cooking of food. Never use kitchen utensils or appliances without adult permission and supervision.

LANGUAGE

English	Norwegian	Sami
Yes	Ja (YAH)	De Lea
No	Nei (NAI)	Li
Thank you	Takk (TAHK)	Giitu
Welcome	Velkommen (vehl-KOM-en)	Buves boahtin
Hello	God dag (go DAHG)	Buorre beaivi
Good-bye	Morn'a (MOARN ah)	Mana dearvan

Economy

Norway's **economy** is based on industry, service, and **petroleum** production. Norway has western Europe's largest petroleum and natural gas fields. Statoil, a government-run company, manages these resources. Norwegian miners dig for copper, iron, and coal. Norwegians also manufacture aluminum, iron, timber, and fish products.

Many Norwegians work as both fishermen and farmers. Norway has about 13,624 miles (21,926 km) of coastline. Each year, Norway's fishing industry catches thousands of pounds of herring, blue whiting, Atlantic cod, prawn, and shrimp.

Very little of Norway's land is good for farming. But Norwegians make the most of this limited area. They grow barley, potatoes, oats, and wheat. Most of

Norway's farmers raise livestock. Norwegian farmers raise cattle, sheep, and pigs.

In addition, forests cover one-fourth of Norway's land. The abundant trees make lumber an important industry. Most of these forests are made up of spruce and pine trees.

Fishing boats and trawlers sail into Stamsund Harbor in the Lofoten Islands.

Urban Norway

King Harald Hardraade (hahr-DRAH-day) founded Oslo in about 1050. In 1624, a fire destroyed the city. King Christian IV had it rebuilt, and gave it the name Christiania. It was renamed Oslo in 1925. Today, it is Norway's capital and largest city.

Oslo is the center of Norway's trade, banking, and shipping industries. Oslo's people produce consumer goods, build ships, and work in the electrical industry. Most of Norway's **cultural** institutions are in Oslo. People visit the National Theatre, the Historical Museum, and the

Buildings at Karl Johans Gate in Oslo

National Gallery. Frogner Park has many sculptures by Gustav Vigeland (GOOS-tahv VEE-guh-lahn).

Oslo is home to the University of Oslo. Founded in 1811, it is the largest and oldest university in Norway. Its library is the main library in the nation.

Bergen is Norway's second-largest city. It lies in southern Norway, and is a main port. Its **economy** is based on fishing, shipbuilding, and machinery and metal manufacturing.

King Olaf III founded Bergen in 1070. It was Norway's capital during the twelfth and thirteenth centuries. The city's oldest structure, the Mary Church, also dates from this time.

A woman sits at the waterfront in Bergen.

Getting Around

Norway has about 56,000 miles (90,123 km) of highways. Most of these roads are paved. Much of Norway's local passenger traffic moves by car. But some people ride buses, too.

More than half of Norway's 2,493 miles (4,012 km) of railways are electrified. Norwegian State Railways runs the railroad. Its trains take people between Norwegian cities, or to other parts of Europe.

Ships are also important in Norway. People ride **ferries** across the **fjords**. Most of the country's freight is transported by ship. Norway has one of the world's largest merchant marines.

For long-distance travel, most Norwegians go by plane. International airlines link Oslo with most major European cities. Oslo is the **junction** of road, rail, and air networks in Norway.

The Floro ferry takes cars and trucks across the Sognefjord.
The fjord is the longest and deepest in Norway.

Norway's one television station is run by the government. It is called the Norwegian Broadcasting Corporation. In Norway, educational programming is more important than entertainment programming.

Government

Norway's government is a **constitutional monarchy**. The government follows the **constitution** of 1814.

Norway's legislative branch consists of a two-house **parliament** called the *Storting* (STOR-tihng). The upper house is called the *Lagting* (LAHG-tihng). The lower house is known as the *Odelsting* (OODEHLS-tihng). The Norwegian people elect *Storting* members to four-year terms. All Norwegians age 18 and over may vote.

A king or queen and a **prime minister** hold executive power. The monarch's power is mostly ceremonial. He or she picks the prime minister and State Council with the agreement of the *Storting*.

Judicial power is held by the Supreme Court. There are also courts of appeal and local courts. But many cases do not go to trial. They are settled in **mediation** councils instead.

Locally, Norway is divided into 19 counties called *fylker* (FIHL-ker). These counties are divided into 448 **municipalities**.

Norway's government has created an excellent social welfare system. Norwegians receive health care, housing assistance, family assistance, **pensions**, and disability from the government.

The Parliament building in Oslo

Holidays & Festivals

Every May 17, Norwegians observe **Constitution** Day. It is the country's biggest holiday. People celebrate with parties, parades, and traditional costumes.

A couple wearing traditional Norwegian clothing practices a dance before a folk festival.

Another popular Norwegian holiday is Midsummer's Eve. It is usually observed on June 23. Norwegians celebrate by building big bonfires on the beach.

On July 29, the people celebrate St. Olaf's Day. It honors King Olaf II Haraldsson, who helped bring Christianity to Norway. He is Norway's patron saint.

Norwegians observe religious holidays, too. Christmas, Ascension Day, and Easter are widely celebrated in Norway. For Easter, the Sami hold colorful festivals in the Karasjok (KAR-ahs-YUHK) and Kautokeino (KOW-tuh-KI-no) communities. The celebrations often include reindeer races and the playing of *joik* (yoyk), a traditional Sami folk music.

A Sami couple dresses in traditional clothing on their wedding day.

Norwegian Culture

Norway has a strong literary tradition. In the thirteenth and fourteenth centuries, poets wrote legends about Viking heroes. The legends wove literary elements with history. The telling of Norse myths and **folktales** is also an old tradition. In recent times, writers Bjørnstjerne Bjørnson (BYORN-steyehrn-eh BYORN-son), Knut Hamsun (KNOOT HAHM-suhn), and Sigrid Undset (SIH-grid OON-set) have each won the Nobel Prize for literature.

Norway's **culture** includes other arts, too. Edvard Munch (ED-vard muhngk) is a famous Norwegian Impressionist painter. His painting *The Cry* is known

Self-Portrait with Wine Bottle *by Edvard Munch*

worldwide. Many of his works are displayed at the Munch Museum in Oslo.

Music is also a part of Norwegian **culture**. One of Norway's famous composers is Edvard Grieg (ED-vard greeg). Much of his music has roots in Norway's folk tradition. He also wrote music for poems and plays, including the *Peer Gynt Suite*.

Edvard Grieg

Skiing in Norway was originally a form of transportation. Today, Norway's long winters and high mountains make skiing the country's national sport. Norway has thousands of miles of cross-country ski trails. Some people even ski in the summer! They ski on the glaciers near Finse (FEENS) and Stryn (STRIHN), and in the Jotunheim (YO-tuhn-haym) Mountains.

A skier competes at the 1994 Winter Olympics, held in Lillehammer, Norway.

In the winter, many ice rinks are filled with skaters. Some skaters play bandy. Bandy is a form of hockey played by two 11-player teams.

In summer, soccer is a favorite sport. Both girls and boys play soccer. Many children also enjoy handball, aerobics, jazz ballet, and swimming.

Norway's literature, arts, and sports reflect the Norwegian people and their beautiful land. The country has grown from a Danish **province** into a strong, independent land.

A woman wearing a traditional Norwegian dress skates at a re-enactment of the Great Ice Fair in Lillehammer, Norway.

A boy runs with the ball at the 16-year-old boys' division of the Norway Cup. Youth teams from around the world come to play at the event each year.

Glossary

Black Death - a deadly disease that spread throughout Europe between 1347 and 1351.

coniferous - a type of tree that has needles or cones, and does not lose its needles in the winter.

constitution - the laws that govern a country.

constitutional monarchy - a form of government ruled by a king or queen who must follow the laws of a constitution.

culture - the customs, arts, and tools of a nation or people at a certain time.

deciduous - a type of tree that loses its leaves in the fall.

economy - the way a city or nation uses its money, goods, and natural resources.

ferry - a boat used to carry people, goods, and cars across a body of water.

fjord - a narrow inlet of the sea with steep slopes or cliffs.

folktale - stories that are a part of the beliefs, traditions, and customs of a people. Folktales are handed down from parent to child.

junction - a place where different paths meet.

mediation - when a third person or group helps two other people or groups to settle an argument.

municipality - a city, town, or other community having self-government.

neutral - not taking sides in a conflict.

parliament - the highest lawmaking body in some governments.

peninsula - land that sticks out into water but is connected to a larger land mass.

pension - money for people to live on after they retire.

petroleum - a thick, yellowish-black oil. It is the source of gasoline.

prime minister - the highest-ranked member of some governments.

province - one of the main divisions of a country.

regent - a person who rules a kingdom during the childhood or absence of the monarch.

seminomad - a member of a people that moves from place to place to find food for their animals, but have a home base where they build homes and grow crops.

social democracy - a political and economic system where the government controls some of the distribution of goods and services. The people elect officials to represent them in the government.

World War II - 1939 to 1945, fought in Europe, Asia, and Africa. The United States, France, Great Britain, the Soviet Union, and their allies were on one side. Germany, Italy, Japan, and their allies were on the other side. The war began when Germany invaded Poland.

Web Sites

Would you like to learn more about Norway? Please visit **www.abdopub.com** to find up-to-date Web site links to more information on the Vikings, the Sami, and the history and culture of Norway. These links are routinely monitored and updated to provide the most current information available.

Index